YOU'RE WORTH IT

FOR GIRLS

SHEILA WALSH

HARVEST HOUSE PUBLISHERS
EUGENE, OREGON

Cover by Design by Julia

Published in association with the literary agency of The FEDD Agency, Inc., PO Box 341973, Austin, TX 78734.

YOU'RE WORTH IT FOR GIRLS

Published by Harvest House Publishers
Eugene, Oregon 97402
www.harvesthousepublishers.com

ISBN 978-0-7369-6387-9 (pbk.)
ISBN 978-0-7369-6388-6 (eBook)

Printed in China

16 17 18 19 20 21 22 23 24 / RDS-JH / 10 9 8 7 6 5 4 3 2 1

Contents

A Message from Sheila: Why You're Worth It! ... 5

1. Picture Time!............................. 11

2. Getting to Know Yourself 19

3. Giving Your Stuff to God.................. 29

4. Being Included 37

5. Getting How Much God Loves You 47

6. Filling Your Heart with God's Truth 57

7. When You Need to Forgive 67

8. God Changes You and Your Life............ 75

9. God Sees Your Heart 83

10. When Things Don't Go Your Way 93

11. Jesus Has a Plan for Your Future 103

Why You're Worth It!

Are not two sparrows sold for a penny?
Yet not one of them will fall to the ground
outside your Father's care. And even the
very hairs of your head are numbered.
So don't be afraid; you are worth
more than many sparrows.
MATTHEW 10:29-31

That was so worth it! If you've ever talked yourself into going on a crazy-fast roller coaster or planned a big sleepover with your friends or helped train your brand-new puppy, you know that certain things in life are totally worth it. They're worth the time and the energy you spend to do them. Going on the roller coaster probably took a *lot* of pumping yourself up. Planning the big sleepover probably took a lot of figuring things out with your parents and friends. And helping train the new puppy? Well, that probably took a lot of time and patience.

You'll always remember these things, though. The things that take the most effort often end up being the best things

5

in life. They allow us to learn. They help us grow. And they become our favorite memories—and our favorite things to talk about! When something is worth it, it's fun to let everyone know all about it, isn't it?

Did you know *you're* one of those things that's worth it? Yes, you are! You're something super special to God. You're one of His favorite things, and you make Him smile. If you didn't know how amazing you are, you're about to find out. You're totally worth it to God, and that's what this book is all about.

God has taken His time and His creativity and His effort to make you and love you and care for you. He's so incredible, He's done this for every single person—ever! It's hard to believe, but it's true.

Together, we're going to discover God's unbelievable love. I'm going to share with you all the ways God has shown me that I'm worth it to Him. And I'm going to show you that you are also worth it!

✵ Totally Loved

You know you're loved, but have you ever felt as if nobody has time for you? Maybe your parents are super busy with work. Or your siblings have too much homework to play with you. Or your best friends are all at summer camp or on vacation, and there's nobody to hang out with. You know your parents and your siblings and your BFFs love you, but sometimes you can feel a little bit lonely. That's perfectly normal. Nobody around you can be there for you 24/7. Nobody can give you 100 percent of their attention all the time.

But wait a second—actually, there *is* Someone who is there for you 24/7. There *is* someone you can talk to any hour of the day—or night. That Someone is God. And here's what's so cool about this: Other people can tell you that you're worth it, but ultimately God is the only One who can make you truly realize that you're worth something.

Your parents can give you hugs and encouragement. Your BFFs can make you cool cards and hand-beaded friendship bracelets. Your piano teacher can fill your practice notebook with "Good job!" stickers and tell you how awesome you're doing in your lessons. But when it comes down to it, those things—as terrific as they are—aren't going to be enough. That's because there's only one source for the kind of love and acceptance all of us crave—and that's in God, the One who made us, and the One who gives us all good things.

Every single girl—and every single person on this planet—has the same exact desire to feel important and worthy and loved. We all want to know that we matter.

If you look at your life, you can see all the ways you matter and all the ways you make a difference. Maybe you're the best helper your teacher has—you love to run classroom errands and help decorate the bulletin board, and you always offer to show new kids around the school. Maybe you're a super big sister who lets your younger siblings play with your stuff and wear your clothes and spend time with you. Maybe you're a terrific teammate who is the first one to give high fives and always listens to your coach. You're really great at these things, and your words and actions do make a difference at school, at home, and on the field.

So definitely keep doing these things. Keep helping your teacher. Continue showing kindness to your siblings. Go right on giving high fives to your teammates. But in the middle of doing all these awesome things, it's really important that you keep focusing on God. That's because your relationship with Him should be the main thing in your life. It's hard to understand that, but just take my word for it. And take His Word—the Bible—for it too!

✳ All the Time

Have you ever felt confused about the choices you have to make? Should you have your best friend over to spend the night, or should you try to get to know some new friends? Should you do art club after school, or should you play a sport? Even little choices—like having peanut butter and apples or chocolate chip cookies for a snack—can be kind of a problem. You know the peanut butter and apples are better for you, but you really *want* chocolate chip cookies!

Because you're so worth it to God, He wants you to talk to Him about everything that's going on in your life. Even your afternoon snack. He's with you *all* the time—24/7—and you have His full attention every moment—100 percent guaranteed! In this book we're going to talk about all the ways God is with you *all the time*. He's with you when...

• you're worried about school or your friendships

- you doubt you can ever do something
- you feel like nobody cares about you
- you feel sad about the things you've said or done
- you're totally confused about absolutely everything

God has always known you. *Always!*
He has always accepted you. *Always!*
He has always loved you. *Always!*
Whether you're feeling confused by your math homework or mad at your brother or sad that your BFF is eating lunch with someone else, you can depend on God to remind you that you're so worth it.

God loves you! No matter what kind of day you're having, remember that *you are worth it—and you are worthy to God*.

God's Word Says You're Worth It

"You created my inmost being; you knit me together in my mother's womb" (Psalm 139:13).

If you have any doubt that God created you to be His amazing, unique, totally worth-it daughter, this is an awesome verse to read and memorize. It proves He was making you *you* even before you were born!

Picture Time!

*We know and rely on the love
God has for us. God is love.
Whoever lives in love lives in
God, and God in them.*

1 JOHN 4:16

Oh, no, Kaitlyn silently groaned. *It's school picture day!*

When she'd gotten on the bus that morning, she hadn't really noticed that the other kids were dressed up. She had wondered a little why her best friend, Faith, had on a dress and was wearing a headband. Faith lived in jeans and T-shirts and always had her hair up in a ponytail or messy bun. But then they'd started talking about their favorite TV show, and Kaitlyn had forgotten all about the dress—until her teacher announced that their class would be taking school pictures right after recess. "So please be careful not to get too messy on the playground."

Kaitlyn had stayed up late eating popcorn and playing Apples to Apples with her family. As a result, she'd slept through her alarm and barely gotten up in time to throw on the sweatshirt she'd worn yesterday (which now had a big stain on the front from her running-out-the-door breakfast of toast and jelly) and the grass-stained jeans she'd worn all weekend. Without bothering to brush her hair, she'd used a hair tie to pull it back from her face. And speaking of brushing…oops! Her toothbrush had gone unused that morning. (She could feel popcorn kernels stuck in her teeth!)

Yep, this school picture day was shaping up to be a big fail! *I hope they have retakes this year*, Kaitlyn thought. *Well, at least I don't have to worry about getting my clothes messed up on the playground. My parents might be mad when they see my pictures, but at least I can play dodgeball.*

✾ ✾ ✾

Kaitlyn didn't plan to show up for school pictures with unbrushed hair tossed up in a hair tie, popcorn kernels stuck in her teeth, and a jelly-stained sweatshirt. And she sure didn't want to bring those pictures home to her parents! But sometimes you just can't help it. You take a bad picture. Maybe your eyes are closed or you have a silly look on your face or your hair is messed up. You're not perfect, so it makes sense that not every picture of you will look perfect.

While most of us don't like looking at bad pictures of ourselves (although, yes, there are those goofballs who will make a silly face on purpose), those pictures are important to see because they tell us the truth about who we are. If we want to see what we really look like, we need to look at *all* the pictures of ourselves—good *and* bad.

I'm not just talking about your physical appearance here—your hair and your smile and your eyes. There are other kinds of pictures that show us what we're like *inside* as well as outside. Making a mean comment to someone else gives others a bad picture of you. So does telling a lie or making up a lame excuse for not doing your homework. On any given day, someone could take hundreds of bad pictures of you—from your unbrushed hair to the gossip you whisper. (And take my word for it, gossip is *way* worse than messy hair.)

And on any given day, someone could take hundreds of *good* pictures of you. Your outfit looks cute and matches. Your smile is happy and real. You're helping a friend with her homework. You're standing up to that bully who picks on your sister. You're giving some of your allowance to the homeless shelter your Sunday school class is helping support. Those are flattering shots. Those are terrific pictures.

If you were to make a photo collage of a real day-in-your-life, it would be made up of good pictures and bad pictures. Everyone's would be! That's because there's no such thing as a Super Girl who always wears the right thing, does the right thing, and says the right thing. If you think your real self needs to be a perfect self, you're totally wrong.

You're not perfect because your world isn't perfect. And guess what? Nobody expects you to be perfect. Even though it may not always seem like it, your parents and your teachers don't expect you to be perfect. And God doesn't expect you to be perfect, either. He just expects you to be *real*. In the next chapter, we're going to get into what it means to be real, but for now just think of the real you as the true you—the you who shows up in every picture (good *or* bad).

✳ The Perfect Picture

Did you know there's only one person who ever lived who would have had a photo album that showed only good pictures? This person never took a bad picture—ever! You may have guessed that this person is Jesus.

Even when people were mean to Him and mocked Him and

MY PHOTO ALBUM

Think back on the week that just happened. What did you do? Where did you go? Who did you talk to? Now, imagine your week happening in a series of photos. First, think about the bad photos (because sometimes you want to get the hard stuff out of the way first). Write down what your top five bad pictures of you might look like (for example, "I talked back to my mom."):

1. _____

2. _____

3. _____

4. _____

5. _____

Now for the positive part! Remember the top five good "pictures" of your week (for example, "I did a great job taking care of my pets all week.") and write them down here:

1. _____

2. _____

3. _____

4. _____

5. _____

Which pictures do you like to look at? Which ones make you feel happy inside? The good ones, right? As you go through the next week, remind yourself that everything you say and do is giving someone a picture—good or bad—of you. While your photo album isn't going to be perfect, you can try to have more good pictures than bad ones. God will help you.

made fun of Him and—I'm totally telling the truth here—spit on Him, He always did the right thing. That's because Jesus is the Son of God. And that's why He was able to live a perfect life on this earth.

Now, like I said before, nobody expects you to be perfect. (Nobody expects anyone to be perfect.) But when you know Jesus—when you talk to Him and read about His life in your Bible and learn more about Him in church—He will help you become more like Him. You'll start seeing things the way He sees things. You'll start loving people the way He loves people. And this is a really important thing! In John 15:12, Jesus says, "My command is this: Love each other as I have loved you."

The Bible is long and can sometimes be hard to understand, but this is really the heart of the whole book. God loves you. And He created you to love Him and to love others. You're worth it to Him. *Everyone* is worth it!

Before we get into what it means to live like Jesus—and for Jesus—it's important to make sure you have accepted Him into your heart and your life. I became a Christian at age 11, and even then it took me some time to understand just how much God loved me. (I'm still learning!) Becoming like Jesus is a lifelong thing, but accepting Him into your life is a decision that everyone needs to make at some point.

If you already know that you're a Christian, awesome! I'm so happy you are also part of the family of God. But if you aren't sure if you're a Christian, or if you want to become a Christian, please talk to one or both of your parents or your Sunday school teacher or another adult you trust. You can also say a prayer like this:

> *Dear Lord,*
>
> *Thank You so much for creating me and loving me. Thank You that I am worth so much to You. I know I have sinned and done and said things I shouldn't have. I also know You sent Jesus to be my Savior, and He died on the cross to set me free from my sins. Please forgive me for all of my sins and come into my life and change my heart. Thank You for always being with me, and*

thank You that I can follow You for the rest of my life and that I will get to live with You in heaven someday. In Jesus' name. Amen.

If you said this prayer for the first time, allow me to give you a (virtual) high five and hug. I'm so excited for you! If you're already a follower of Jesus, I'm also excited for you. And if you aren't quite sure, I'm excited to have you keep reading and join me on this journey.

If I were you, the picture I'd put on page one of your photo album is a picture of you and Jesus. He's holding your hand and guiding you every step of the way as you go to school, hang out at home, and go do stuff in the world. He'll always be there for you—*always*! That's because you're so worth it to Him.

❋ DISCOVER YOUR WORTH ❋

Stop for a minute and think about what a photo album of your life might look like. Would it have more good pictures, more bad pictures, or about the same amount of both? If you wish you could get rid of the bad pictures, you can pray and ask God to forgive you for some of the things you've said or done. Then tell Him you want a photo album filled with *good* pictures— pictures that show you as a girl who loves Jesus and is trying to be like Him. He'll help you do this. You're worth it to Him!

God's Word Says You're Worth It

*"Whoever claims to live in him must
live as Jesus did" (1 John 2:6).*

The best way to be sure we have more good pictures than bad
pictures of ourselves is to try to be like Jesus. The Bible says
that if we say we are a Christian, we need to act like one too.
It's important to do our best to be like Jesus.

Getting to Know Yourself

*You have searched me, LORD,
and you know me.*

PSALM 139:1

This is so hard, thought Lindy. *I love both of my parents, and I know they love me, but I feel caught in the middle sometimes. I want to visit my dad on the weekends, but that means I miss stuff with my friends. I know my dad tries to make me feel comfortable, but it's not easy switching back and forth. Sometimes I feel like I don't really know who I am...*

Lindy's parents had gotten divorced when she was eight, and she'd spent the past two years traveling back and forth between her mom's house and her dad's apartment in a different town. She usually spent weekends and a lot of the summer with her dad, and he did his best to make things comfortable and fun, but it was just...different. A different room. Different food. Different feelings. To be honest, Lindy felt a little bit like a different person when she was at her dad's.

Her parents were really good about not putting a lot of pressure on her. When Lindy had a tap dance recital or a birthday party on the weekend, her parents made sure everything worked out just right. But she didn't like driving back and forth, and she didn't like trying to fit in her weekend homework—when she had it—around the schedules of two different families.

Now that I know Jesus and know that He loves me too, it's kind of getting better, Lindy thought. *But it's still tough being a kid of divorced parents. I try to be myself, but sometimes I don't know who the real Lindy is.*

* * *

Like a lot of kids whose parents are divorced, Lindy was struggling to figure out who she was. Of course, she was always Lindy! But with two different homes and two different ways of doing things, it makes sense that things were kind of confusing. Even if their parents *aren't* divorced, it can be hard for kids to figure out who they really are.

You have a different mix of kids in your class every year. A different teacher every grade. Your hobbies and interests change. Are you a swimmer or a dancer? A piano player or an artist? Who exactly *are* you?

When I was younger my father died and my family went through a hard time. I was a little confused about who I really was. Because I'd lost my dad, I was sometimes scared that I was going to do something or say something to make God not love me anymore and lose His love, too. Now, this was totally untrue. God *always* loves His children! But I wasn't sure, so I prayed about it. And God answered my prayer when I read one of my favorite parts of His Word, Psalm 91. You can read the whole psalm on your own, but the beginning of it is what really helped me learn to trust God:

> Whoever dwells in the shelter of the Most High
> will rest in the shadow of the Almighty. I will say
> of the LORD, "He is my refuge and my fortress,
> my God, in whom I trust" (Psalm 91:1-2).

When I read this psalm today, it still reminds me of the love and protection God gives me—even when I'm scared and confused and trying to figure out who I am. This psalm helped me realize and truly believe that God's love for me was real and unchanging. Even if I wasn't perfect and life wasn't perfect, God still cared about me.

Like Lindy, maybe your parents are divorced. Maybe some of your relatives don't talk to each other. Or maybe some of your friends are having family problems—and that's affecting your friendship. When things like this are happening, you need to trust God that He will take care of you and that He will help the grown-ups around you sort things out. He promises to take care of you, and you can talk to Him about absolutely anything. He sees the true you—all of your worries and hopes and dreams and thoughts and feelings. And He loves the true you!

WHO ARE YOU?

From your favorite song to your favorite color to your favorite book, you have your own set of "likes" that's not like anybody else's. Take a moment to celebrate being *you* by writing down your very favorite things:

- Favorite song: _____

- Favorite book: _____

- Favorite color: _____

- Favorite sport or activity: _____

- Favorite Bible verse: _____

- Favorite animal: _____

- Favorite place to go on vacation: _____

It will be fun to look back at this list in six months or a year to see if these are still your favorite things. Remember, you're always growing and changing, and that's perfectly normal. So thank God for making you *you* and celebrate who you are now—and who you're becoming!

✻ Your Real Self

Lindy's struggle was her family situation. I also had trouble with my family situation when I was a kid. I don't know what your struggle is. Maybe it's a learning disability that makes it hard for you to do your schoolwork. Or you're really shy, and it's not easy for you to make new friends. You may even have a physical challenge that makes it tough for you to get involved in things. Whatever your struggle is, don't try to run away from it or pretend it's not there. It's part of your real self, and God loves the real you!

Now, this next part may be hard, but I encourage you to take this important step: Get to know and accept your real self. You do this by accepting that whatever you're dealing with is a part of you, and then you pray and ask God—who totally accepts you, no matter what—to help you love and accept yourself.

If you're struggling with a physical or a learning challenge, go to God and ask Him how you can honor Him with that challenge. Ask Him who in your life might be inspired and encouraged by you.

If it's shyness you're dealing with, ask God to help you accept that your shyness is part of who you are. Maybe you take longer to make friends, but the friends you have are really terrific, close friends.

Maybe you're being bullied at school. Or your mom lost her job. Or a grandparent is in the hospital. You can feel forgotten and lost in the middle of all these problems, and you can easily start feeling that you aren't worth very much or you don't really matter. But you are. And you do!

THE REAL ME— MY FEELINGS

It's hard to feel that we're worth it when we have lots of negative feelings inside of us. Circle or highlight the things you sometimes feel, and then take a look at what God says about you instead.

My Feeling: I'm just a kid. I'm not important.

God's Feeling: Everyone matters to Me, no matter how old they are. You are important!

My Feeling: I wish I were cuter. I feel ugly when I look in the mirror.

God's Feeling: I created you, and you are amazingly beautiful!

My Feeling: I'm worried about lots of stuff—my family, my schoolwork, my friendships.

God's Feeling: You can trust Me with all of your problems. You can give your worries to Me.

My Feeling: I feel like such a loser! Everyone else is so much better than me.

God's Feeling: I created you to be one-of-a-kind and unique. You're perfect just the way you are!

My Feeling: I'm ashamed of the way I treat other people. I want to be nice, but sometimes I just can't help the words that come out of my mouth.

God's Feeling: I know you're not perfect, and I love and accept you anyway! You can always come to Me when you feel like you need help.

My Feeling: I'm lonely. Nobody likes me, and I don't have any real friends.

God's Feeling: I'm always there for you! And I will bring the best kind of friends into your life.

My Feeling: Sometimes I get upset about stuff that shouldn't matter, and I don't even know why.

God's Feeling: Your emotions are natural, and that's okay. I can give you peace and joy. I can fill your life with My love.

From our biggest problems to our smallest mistakes, God really gets us. And that's why He encourages us to go to Him in prayer for our every need. We can just plop down on a chair and start talking to Him. It's really that easy! And God will always listen to us because we matter to Him.

If you're looking for a good starting place to begin talking to God, try praying Psalm 91 like I did. It's impossible to read this psalm without pausing from verse to verse and thinking about God's love for you. The God of Psalm 91 is described as our shelter, our refuge, and our strength. That's super powerful! I'm so grateful that as a young girl I believed in God's great love for me. That truth has always stuck with me and has helped me more than I ever imagined it would.

If you're struggling with your feelings or your faith or anything else, I encourage you to pray the same kind of prayer I prayed when I was asking God to help me with the stuff I was going through.

> *Father God,*
>
> *I trust that You want to help me. I know that if You wanted to, You could immediately take away all of my problems and make everything totally better in my life. But even if You choose not to do that, I will still thank You and praise You—even though that might be hard to do! I thank You that You are good and You are God, all the time. All the time! Amen.*

We can't allow our problems to affect our worth before God. If we let that happen, none of us would be worth anything because all of us have problems. I can promise you that none of the girls you know are perfect—even the ones who seem like they are. But I also promise you that every single person— including *you*—is worthy and worth it. God says so!

❧ DISCOVER YOUR WORTH ❧

As you're getting to know your real self, think about the things that may be holding you back from believing you're worth it to God. You may use words like *failure*, *fear*, *lack of confidence*, shyness, emotions, gossip, bad experiences, or a thousand others. Then ask God to show you how much He loves you and how much He takes care of you. Read Psalm 91 again to see how much He cares for you!

God's Word Says You're Worth It

"God so loved the world that he gave his one and only Son, that whoever believes in him shall not perish but have eternal life" (John 3:16).

Everyone in the whole world is worth it to God. It's important to know this because once you believe it, it will be a lot easier to love and accept other people—even the people who don't seem that lovable. They're worthy and worth it, and so are you!

3

Giving Your Stuff to God

I the LORD search the heart and examine the mind, to reward each person according to their conduct, according to what their deeds deserve.

JEREMIAH 17:10

Elizabeth grabbed a few more sweatshirts out of the drawer and set them on her bed. *That should do it,* she thought. *You never know if it's going to be cold at night. Oh, wait! Socks. I totally forgot socks.* She added eight pairs of socks to the growing pile on her bed—and then she threw in two pairs of wool socks just in case it got really cold at night.

Packing for summer camp was a challenge. She and her best friend were going to their church's sleepaway camp for a whole week, and Elizabeth wanted to make sure she wasn't forgetting anything. Judging from the mountain of clothes on her bed and the empty drawers in her dresser, she wasn't in much danger of forgetting anything at all.

Stuffing T-shirts and shorts and fleece pullovers into her giant duffel bag, Elizabeth wondered if she'd even be able to lift

29

it. And sure enough, once everything was packed—including her Bible, her journal, an extra journal in case she ran out of room in the first one, a set of her favorite pens (because she couldn't choose just one color), a few more swimsuits in case her favorite swimsuit took too long to dry, and an extra pillow and blanket in case she didn't like the ones in the cabin—her bag was impossible to lift.

"Mom!" called Elizabeth. "Help! I can't pick up my bag. I've got too much stuff."

❊ ❊ ❊

Have you ever loaded up your duffel bag or backpack or sports bag with so much stuff you could barely lift it? (Maybe you *couldn't* lift it and had to leave some of the items behind—like I think Elizabeth might need to.) When you were packing, it didn't look like *that* much stuff—until you tried to pick it up. And failed.

And it's not just the stuff we carry in bags and backpacks that can be too heavy for us to pick up. Did you know you can carry around stuff on the *inside* that other people never see? We can carry around things like worry. And fear. And sadness. That stuff can really bother us. It can make us feel anxious all the time. It can mess up our sleep. It can affect our relationships with our friends and with our family.

Trying to carry too much stuff isn't good for us. And trying to hide that we're carrying too much stuff can make things even worse. Sometimes I find myself trying to carry around too much stuff all by myself. I forget to ask others for help. I even forget to ask God. When I do this, here's what He says to me: *I love you, My daughter, more than you'll ever realize. And all the extra stuff that's weighing you down is just a reminder that your strength and purpose and worth come from Me, not from yourself or from others. I will help you!*

God wants to help you carry your stuff. And He wants you to know that others—like your parents or your favorite aunt or your small-group leader—can help you carry it too. Isn't that nice to know? You don't have to carry that big heavy bag all by yourself—you don't have to carry any part of it. You can give it all to God, and He will carry it for you. He'll have others carry it for you too. And He may even get rid of some of the stuff you don't really need!

❋ God's Grace

You've probably heard a lot about grace in church or Sunday school or just when you're reading the Bible. It can be a little hard to understand, but what it boils down to is this: Nothing we do or say will ever make God love us more or less. Jesus died on the cross to free us from our sins, and we don't have to do anything to receive His love. We don't have to try to be something we're not or freak out that God will ever stop loving us.

God knows the real you. And He loves—*cherishes*—you anyway. He knows your deepest feelings, the things you long for, the dreams you have. He knows all the mistakes you've made and all the things others have done to hurt you. He knows you so well!

PACKING LIST

Pretend you're going camping by yourself for a whole week. (I know, your parents would never let you go camping by yourself, but just pretend here.) Write down absolutely everything you think you'll need for the trip—and I mean *everything*.

_____

_____

_____

_____

_____

Now pretend your family decided to come along with you—which is probably a good idea. Cross off anything they can bring and just leave your own stuff on the list. You'll have a lot less packing to do, won't you?

God was there for me when I was a young girl and my family was having problems, and He's been there for me so many other times. He didn't always change things right away, but never once has He been absent from my life. Never once was His love for me less than I needed. No matter what was happening to me, God was there holding my hand and loving me and understanding every little part of my life. And He was carrying the stuff that was too heavy for me to lift all by myself.

❊ The Woman at the Well

I love reading stories in the Bible about Jesus helping different types of people. He even ministered to women, which may not seem weird to you, but you have to understand that it was kind of weird back then. In those days, men and women didn't really talk to each other casually. Maybe at your school kids in the older grades don't talk much to kids in the younger grades. Or kids in certain groups or cliques don't hang out with each other. It was kind of like that.

One of my favorite stories of Jesus ministering to a woman is found in John 4. It's such a great story! We never find out the woman's name, but the Bible refers to her as the Samaritan woman, so that's what we'll call her here.

The Samaritan woman had made some bad choices in her life. We're not sure why she made those choices, but as a result people didn't really want to hang out with her. By the time Jesus met her, she was carrying around a lot of extra stuff, didn't really have any friends or family, and wasn't exactly a happy camper.

The Bible says she went to a well to get water at the sixth hour, which is noon by the Palestinian clock. That was the time of day when the sun was at its hottest—and believe me, it got super hot there! She chose that hour to go to the well because none of the other women from the village would be there. She didn't want to see people whispering and gossiping about her. She didn't want anyone to come up to her and say mean things or make fun of her.

STUFF IN MY BAG

What are some of the things *you're* carrying around inside? Circle or highlight the words that apply to you, or write down your own thing if it's not listed here:

fear   sadness   frustration   disappointment

guilt   worry   anxiety   boredom

anger   confusion   lack of confidence

If you want to, you can even write these things down on separate little pieces of paper. The next thing to do is to give these feelings and emotions to God. Just say out loud, "God, I give You my sadness," or "Jesus, I give You my anxiety." Then cross the word out (or, if you've used a separate piece of paper, you can crumple up the word and throw it in the trash). It's gone—you've given it to God!

Think about it this way. Have you ever messed up or done something embarrassing and wished you could just disappear on the spot? That's how the Samaritan woman felt every day! She just wanted to be by herself. She knew that everyone knew all about her bad choices, but she didn't want to be reminded of them.

Have you ever carried a full bucket of water? It's heavy—really heavy! The well the Samaritan woman went to was about half a mile from her home village. So she had to walk half a mile with a full bucket of water at the hottest part of the day. Wow. She really did go out of her way to make sure she didn't see anyone she knew.

She was pretty shocked when she met Jesus that day at the well. For one thing, He started talking to her. She didn't know Him *and* He was a man, so that was strange. Besides, He was a rabbi—or a teacher—so it was expected that He would never, ever talk to a woman in public.

There's even more to the story. Jesus was a Jew, and the woman was a Samaritan. Back then, the Jews couldn't stand the Samaritans, but Jesus talked to her anyway. And what He told her was basically this: "I know how you've been living your life. You've been married five times and now you're living with a man you're not married to. You're carrying around too much stuff."

Did Jesus say this to make the woman feel bad about herself?

Was He mad at her?

Not at all! He told her these things because He loved her. He needed her to know that He knew all about her and that He could help her carry the things that were too heavy for her to carry all by herself.

And the same goes for you and me. Unless we believe that Jesus knows each embarrassing little secret we keep and loves us anyway, we'll never understand how much He loves us.

God is aware of every mistake you've ever made, every problem you've ever had, every embarrassing moment you've ever experienced. And He is *still* happy to see you and talk to you and carry your way-too-heavy bag for you. You're worth it to Him!

❁ DISCOVER YOUR WORTH ❁

Are you starting to get the message that you're worth it to God? We all are! And even though we're all worth it, all of our stories are not the same. We all have different stuff in our bags, but we all struggle to carry that stuff. When you're feeling that your bag is too heavy—when you feel sad or anxious or worried—share your feelings with God. Praise Him for how awesome He is, and then hand over your too-heavy bag and allow Him to carry it for you.

God's Word Says You're Worth It

"He died for all, that those who live should no longer live for themselves but for him who died for them and was raised again" (2 Corinthians 5:15).

If you have any doubt at all how much you're worth to God, just think about the fact that He sent His Son, Jesus, to die on the cross to take away your sins and give you eternal life. Wow! What an amazing way to show His great love for you.

4

Being Included

Blessed are the poor in spirit, for theirs is the kingdom of heaven. Blessed are those who mourn, for they will be comforted. Blessed are the meek, for they will inherit the earth.

MATTHEW 5:3-5

"Are you doing okay, honey?" Lilly's mom asked as Lilly shoved toast and scrambled eggs around and around on her plate. "At least have some juice. You need to eat something."

"I'm not that hungry, Mom," Lilly replied. "My stomach kind of hurts. I'll probably feel better by lunch, but I'm just a little nervous right now."

"Well, at least take a granola bar. Maybe you'll feel like eating something on the way. We should get going in a few minutes." Lilly's mom handed Lilly her favorite flavor of granola bar—chocolate-chip-cherry—and hugged her daughter.

Lilly never liked starting new things, but today was the biggest new thing of all—starting at a brand-new school. And not only that, but this was a brand-new school in a brand-new state. Her dad had taken a new job all the way across the country, and Lilly had no idea what school would be like here. Would the math be too hard? Would her clothes look okay? Would the other kids think she seemed different?

The thought of starting at a new school with absolutely no friends at all terrified Lilly. The kids she had met in Sunday school the past few weeks either went to other schools or to private school or were homeschooled.

"Mom?" Lilly said, putting the granola bar in her backpack. "Can we pray about this? I'm more scared than I thought I would be..."

✳ ✳ ✳

Starting something new is never, ever easy. Whether it's a new school or a new activity or just meeting a new friend, there's always a period of awkwardness and discomfort. A lot of our uneasiness comes from our desire to fit in. We're scared we won't find other kids similar to us or friends who we connect with. And we're also terrified deep down (or maybe not so deep down!) that nobody will talk to us or want to be our friend. We worry that we won't say or do the right thing.

When we so desperately want to be included, it's hard to face rejection. And it seems as though there are so many situations where rejection is a major possibility—especially when we find ourselves as the new kid like Lilly was. Maybe you're used to eating lunch with your two best friends every single day. Then, one day, both of them are home sick. Do you go up to a new group of kids—and risk not being included—or do you just eat alone?

SOMEONE SPECIAL

Sometimes, when we're scared we won't be included, things that aren't true pop into our head. Do any of these thoughts sound familiar?

You'll never amount to anything.

You'll never be as cute or as smart as other girls.

You're not very good at making friends.

Your parents like your sister (or your brother) better than you.

None of these things are true, but sometimes we get really down on ourselves. When you notice this is happening, stop yourself right there and say, "Hey, that's not true! I'm really good at lots of things. Lots of people want to be my friend. I'm worth it to God, so that means I'm someone special.

Or it's tryout time for your soccer club. You're scared that other kids are better than you, so do you risk rejection and try out anyway or just quit soccer? And what about the big stuff—like moving to a new city or attending a new church or going to a new school—where you have to start over completely?

Like Lilly, sometimes we're more scared than we thought we would be.

✺ The Beauty of a Cracked Mug

When I was a student in London (yep, I'm British), one of my favorite places to shop was the Reject China Shop. Seriously, that's what it was called. It was next to Harrods, a very fancy department store where *nothing* is a reject. The Reject China Shop sold the cups and dishes and mugs that weren't perfect enough to be sold at Harrods. As a student with not very much money, I admired the china Harrods sold, but I did my shopping next door to save money.

One day I went into the Reject China Shop on a mission to find a perfect mug that had slipped in by mistake. I held mug after mug up to the light, but each time I would see a chip or a flaw, a tiny crack beneath the glaze. But then—*jackpot*! I found a piece that looked perfect. Feeling as though I'd won the lottery, I bought the mug and took it home.

The minute my tea water had boiled, I poured it into the mug and watched in disbelief as a crack suddenly appeared from top to bottom. It had been impossible to see until the heat exposed it. My new mug wasn't perfect, after all. It was about to fall apart!

Did you know every single person is like my mug? Some people may look perfect—like they have no problems at all. They're not worried about being the new kid or scared they won't make the soccer team. But nobody's perfect. Everyone has some flaws and cracks and chips. And without Jesus, we can fall apart.

We all need Jesus in our lives. His love makes us worth it. Nothing else matters!

Have you ever felt like something from the Reject China Shop? We all have! You might feel that you're not as pretty as your best friend. Or that your sister is so much better at playing the piano. Or that your brother is so much smarter than you.

When you catch yourself thinking like this, stop! Remember that God loves you and is always there for you. He'll always pick you up when you're down on yourself. Romans 8:31 says, "What, then, shall we say in response to these things? If God is for us, who can be against us?"

If God is on your side, you're always included! No matter how many times you feel rejected, God's arms are always open, always loving, always there for you.

Now, I'm not saying rejection isn't real. It is. I'm also not saying rejection doesn't hurt. It does. In a lot of situations, there's a winner and a loser—from a softball game to a dance competition to even Bible quizzing. Not everyone is going to get first place. Not everyone is going to get the best grade. Not everyone is going to win the art contest. I can tell you over and over that these things don't really matter, but the reality is that they do. Losing stings. Rejection hurts.

Sometimes, when you're feeling especially sad or lonely, consider that Jesus Himself felt rejected from His own people. John 1:11 says, "He came to that which was his own, but his own did not receive him." Yes, even Jesus understands rejection!

Remember that God chooses broken mugs—which all of us are—to fill with His ever-flowing love and acceptance.

TURN YOUR NEGATIVES INTO POSITIVES

Words are powerful! The words others tell you, along with the words you tell yourself, will help form your sense of identity. When someone criticizes you, don't immediately tell yourself, *They're right. I'm terrible at this. I'm not worth anything.* Instead, learn to turn what you hear as a negative into a positive. I'll give you some examples:

- A classmate says, "You're not finished reading that yet? You are so slow!" Tell yourself: "I'm not the fastest reader around, but I'm a really careful reader. I can remember a lot of information because I really think about what I'm reading as I read it."

- A teammate says, "You've only run three laps? I already finished my fourth lap!" Tell yourself: "I'm not a sprinter, but I do work super hard and I'm getting faster. And I can keep on running when everyone else is exhausted!"

- A girl on the playground says, "Why do you dress like that? Nobody else wears dresses to school!" Tell yourself: "I like my sense of style, and I like being my own person. Dresses are cute and they look cute on me. Plus, in some schools, most girls wear dresses."

Once you start doing this, it becomes a fun game. And it's actually kind of addictive. Soon you'll find yourself listening to negative comments that people are making about others (which is a nasty thing called *gossip*) and turning those negatives into positives. You can even say them out loud (cheerfully and with a smile, of course) and change the way other kids think about themselves and about each other. Isn't that awesome?

❁ Dive into God's Deep Love

The best way to remind yourself that you're included and worth it is to see what the Bible says about God's acceptance of you. And then tell yourself over and over that God loves you and accepts you and that you're worth it to Him. You can use some of my favorite verses to help you believe this:

> Though my father and mother forsake me, the LORD will receive me (Psalm 27:10).

> You created my inmost being; you knit me together in my mother's womb. I praise you because I am fearfully and wonderfully made; your works are wonderful, I know that full well. My frame was not hidden from you when I was made in the secret place, when I was woven together in the depths of the earth (Psalm 139:13-15).

> God demonstrates his own love for us in this: While we were still sinners, Christ died for us (Romans 5:8).

Take some time to think about God's loving words to you. Read them over and over. Say them out loud. Memorize them. Write them down in your journal. They're the truth—God's overwhelming love for you. For *you*! After all, it wasn't just for "the world" that Christ died. It was for *you*. God has placed a value on your life and that value is the life of Christ. Every single one of us is worth to God the most valuable possession of all—His Son.

If that isn't amazing, I don't know what is!

✻ DISCOVER YOUR WORTH ✽

We've talked about being rejected and being included in this chapter. Whenever you start to feel rejected, think of the verses I shared in this chapter and tell yourself, "God accepts me. I'm worth it!" Then think of all the ways you can let other people know they're accepted. Acceptance is something you want to share!

God's Word Says You're Worth It

"We love because he first loved us" (1 John 4:19).

God was the first One to accept us—which He did before we were even born—and that's the best reason of all to love and accept other people. If you're finding it hard to love someone, just remind yourself that God loved them first. And He will help you!

Getting How Much God Loves You

See what great love the Father has lavished on us, that we should be called children of God! And that is what we are!

1 JOHN 3:1

No way! thought McKenzie as she saw the giant—and we're talking really giant—wrapped package sitting in the living room. *It can't be!*

But when she took off the wrapping paper (well, the sheets that were serving as wrapping paper), she saw that it was what she'd been wanting. Ever since she'd tried paddleboarding at camp, McKenzie had been begging for a beginner paddleboard of her own. She knew they weren't cheap—even a kid's version was pretty expensive—so she didn't really expect to get one. But here it was—in her favorite shade of green and sitting in the living room.

"Happy birthday, McKenzie!" said her older brother. "Surprised?"

"What do you think?" McKenzie grinned, reading the birthday card. "Oh, wow! All of you went in on it together!"

"Hey, it made birthday shopping easy," her dad said, laughing. "A bunch of relatives sent money, and having five older siblings sometimes comes in handy. Ready to head for the lake?"

"Yes!" McKenzie exclaimed. "And everyone gets a turn on it. Except the birthday girl gets to go first! I still can't believe you guys got me this. No way did I think I would get a paddleboard. Thanks, guys!"

❃ ❃ ❃

Have you ever received a gift that was a total surprise? Maybe you put something big on your birthday list—like McKenzie's paddleboard—and thought, *There's no way I'm ever going to get this*. But then your parents and your grandparents and some other relatives pooled their money and bought you that very thing. Or a friend gave you a present just because. No special reason. She just felt like it.

When we get gifts we weren't expecting, it's really exciting. But there's also another feeling that comes along with the excitement—disbelief. *Really?* we wonder. *Is this truly for me? I don't think I deserve it.*

But you do deserve it! Somebody thought you were worth it. McKenzie's family thought she was worth it. Whenever anyone gives you a gift or a hug or does something kind for you, that person thinks you're worth it. And guess who else thinks you're worth it? God does!

Sometimes it's hard to understand—and receive—God's amazing love. It seems too good to be true. But hang in there and keep praying and reading your Bible and learning and growing. When you finally "get" how much God loves you, you won't believe it. (Well, you *will* believe it. And that's what's so amazing!)

It's awesome that you're reading this right now and learning how much God loves you and how much He thinks you're worth. A lot of people live their entire lives not understanding how much God loves them, and I really wish they could have known that earlier. I remember talking with an older woman who had been attending church and Bible studies her entire life but only recently realized how much God loved her. She told me, "I finally understand for the first time that God really loves me. It's just that simple. He loves me!"

I love how she said this. It *is* simple! But what happens is huge. The power of God's love for each of us is life-changing. You go from seeing yourself as just another girl wandering around on the planet to seeing yourself as God's specially chosen daughter whom He loves more than any earthly father has ever loved a daughter.

WISH LIST

Just for fun, think of absolutely everything you could ever want for your next birthday and for Christmas. Dream big! Write down your top ten "wants" here:

1. _____

2. _____

3. _____

4. _____

5. _____

6. _____

7. _____

8. _____

9. _____

10. _____

God's love is worth way more than everything on your list, and He's already given that to you. He's also given you forgiveness for your sins and eternal life. Talk about dream gifts!

❄ God's Perfect Love

When I was a young girl, my dad had a hard time showing his love because he had a brain injury. I don't know what your situation is like. Maybe you have a great dad who makes you feel loved and special. I wish every girl could experience that kind of family, but the reality is that not everyone does. Maybe your parents are divorced and you don't see your dad very often. Maybe your dad is a single father who does his best, but it's hard for him to do everything on his own. Maybe your dad travels a bunch for his work, and you wish he was home more. Every girl's situation is different, but we all have one thing in common: We all have parents who love us, but we also have a God who loves us even more!

Did you know that the love of a good earthly father is a picture of our heavenly Father's love? Think of how a good dad loves his daughter. He plays with her. He teaches her to throw a ball or plant a garden. He helps her with her homework. He gives her an allowance and buys her little treats. He corrects her when she makes mistakes. He hugs her and comforts her when she's feeling sad.

A good father/daughter relationship shows us a glimpse of the even greater love God has for us. How lucky all of us are to have such a loving heavenly Father.

God's love for you is totally perfect. He never has a hard time showing His love. He's never too busy to listen to your prayers. He's always there for you. I know it's hard to think about God hearing the prayers of everyone on earth. It's hard enough for us to try to watch TV and do our homework, much less listen to just two separate conversations at once. But God can do it because…well, He is God. He can do anything!

✵ Soooo Thirsty!

Have you ever been so thirsty that you think you're going to die if you don't get something to drink? If you're out riding your bike on a 100-degree day, a cup of hot cocoa (even with whipped cream and sprinkles!) isn't going to satisfy your thirst. You need a big glass of ice-cold water or lemonade.

Do you remember the woman at the well—the one who went to fetch water in the noonday sun and walked half a mile back to her village with the super heavy water bucket? When she was at the well, Jesus told her, "Everyone who drinks this water will be thirsty again, but whoever drinks the water I give them will never thirst. Indeed, the water I give them will become a spring of water welling up to eternal life" (John 4:13-14).

Jesus was saying that everyone who drinks the actual water from the well will be thirsty again. Your body needs water every day to stay healthy. But the living water that Jesus gives will be enough to satisfy anyone's inner thirst. Nothing can take the place of God's love, and once you have that, you don't need anything more.

I've spent a lot of my life thirsting for God's love, and He refreshes me every day. His love never runs out. I'm so happy I was able to discover God's love for me!

There are so many terrific things about God's love, but possibly the most important thing I've learned about it is this: *His love doesn't depend on me.* There's nothing I can do to make God love me more, and there's nothing I can do to make Him love me less. His love is perfect. It's endless. It's unchanging. It has nothing to do with me—how I act, what I say, what I do. It has everything to do with God. And remember—it's simple. *God loves me!*

One of my favorite verses about God's love is Romans 8:38-39:

> I am convinced that neither death nor life, neither angels nor demons, neither the present nor the future, nor any powers, neither height nor depth, nor anything else in all creation, will be able to separate us from the love of God that is in Christ Jesus our Lord.

I love to reread these verses. They are such a great reminder that nothing I do or say can ever separate me from God's love. God doesn't only love me if I ace my vocabulary test. He doesn't only love me if I put away the dishes. He doesn't only love me if I read my Bible every morning. He loves me all the time!

Sometimes what's happening in your life affects how you feel about yourself and how you feel about God's love toward you. If things are great with friends and at school and at home, you're probably pretty happy with yourself. It's easy to think, *Of course God loves me. Things are going great. His love is so obvious.*

But when you fail in some area of your life, you may

wrongly believe God's love for you has changed. When this happens, you need to remember that God doesn't give us His love because of what we've done or not done. In fact, God gives us His love *in spite of* what we've done or not done. God has seen our every mistake, our every bad thought, our every failure—and He still loves us! His love is that amazing. That deep. That incredible. You deserve the gift of God's love because you're worth it!

❀ DISCOVER YOUR WORTH ❀

It's one thing to learn about God's love for you. But all the learning in the world doesn't matter unless you actively *receive* that love. I would love for you to pray this prayer of acceptance of God's love for you. You can even pray it out loud with a parent of someone else close to you.

> *Heavenly Father, it's hard for me to understand Your love for me. And it's also hard for me to know how to accept it. But now, by faith, I totally accept Your love for me. I believe Jesus has taken away my every sin. Help me to know You more and to grow deeper and deeper in Your love. Please don't ever let me forget or doubt that You value me as highly as the life of Your Son. Amen.*

God's Word Says You're Worth It

"The LORD your God is with you, the Mighty Warrior who saves. He will take great delight in you; in his love he will no longer rebuke you, but will rejoice over you with singing" (Zephaniah 3:17).

The love of God is the best gift we could ever hope to receive! It's such an amazing gift that sometimes it's easy to feel like we don't deserve it. But we do—because God says so. So accept the gift of His love and start celebrating!

6

Filling Your Heart with God's Truth

Guide me in your truth and teach me,
for you are my God and Savior, and
my hope is in you all day long.

PSALM 25:5

Noooo! Not another true or false quiz! Caroline squeezed her pencil and drummed her feet on the floor. *These are always so confusing!*

Caroline wasn't a big fan of tests, but she especially didn't like true or false tests. Multiple choice tests were okay. You could usually eliminate a few answers, and that gave you a pretty good chance at figuring out the correct one. But true or false? You had a 50/50 chance of getting it right, which also meant you had a 50/50 chance of getting it wrong.

Plus Caroline was always worried that the teacher was trying to trick her (especially her teacher this year!). And sometimes the false answer kind of made sense. Or when she was taking the test—and freaking out and thinking about it way too much—it did make sense.

Caroline slowly started filling in the answers, going back

and erasing this answer and rethinking that answer. By the time the bell rang, she still hadn't finished the test. She hurriedly filled in the last two answers, put her test on the teacher's desk, and then slumped out of the classroom.

"That was so easy!" she heard one of the other kids exclaim. "I love true or false tests. I hate it when we have to write out our answers."

Not me, Caroline thought. *Give me a fill-in-the-blanks test any day. True or false tests are so confusing!*

✿ ✿ ✿

If you're like Caroline and have a hard time figuring out true and false tests, I have some good news for you. God's truth is easy to believe! In His Word, He clearly tells us what is true so we can fill our hearts with His truth.

Sometimes, though, things happen that make it a little bit hard for us to figure out what is the truth and what is a lie. You may be going through a hard time with your friendships, trying to figure out who is a true friend and who isn't. That's really common with girls your age as they start discovering who they are. Or a friend has different rules in her house than you have in yours, and you're wondering what you should do when you play at her house.

It basically comes down to recognizing the difference between right and wrong, which can be hard sometimes when you hear different things from different people. So how can you know what the real truth—God's truth—is? Here are some of my favorite ways of figuring it out:

- Read your Bible. (You can even read it out loud. It's good for us to *hear* the Word of God.)

- Write out your favorite Bible verses and post them everywhere—in your room, on your bathroom mirror, on your walls. You can even paint them on a canvas that you buy in a craft store.

- Look for specific verses about God's love and truth. A great place to start is the Psalms. I find so much encouragement in them.

- Buy a great devotional—one written for girls your age—and go through it with your best friend or your mom or dad.

- Pray! Ask God to reveal the truth to you. He promises to help you.

✤ What's the Deal with the Truth?

So what's the big deal with truth? Shouldn't you just do what you feel like doing and hope everything works out okay? Um...not really! Knowing God's truth makes life a whole lot easier. When you know God's truth, you'll be able to spot something false a mile away.

Let me give you an example. The Bible says a lot about friendships and how we should treat other people.

IT'S ALL IN HOW YOU THINK

Did you know that how you think about God affects your life in a major way? Thinking about God the correct way allows you to know who God really is. And it allows you to learn His truth better.

- If you think God is someone who doesn't care about a kid like you, that thought will make it hard for you to receive His love.

- If you think God keeps track of all your mistakes and gets upset with you when you mess up, that thought will keep you from enjoying His love.

- If you think God plays favorites, that thought will affect how you pray. If one of your prayers seems like it's not being answered, you may think that God loves other people more than He loves you.

If, however, you think God loves you with all His heart on your good days as well as your not-so-good days, then you'll better understand who He is. And you'll better understand His truth and His Word. So start thinking about it!

Take a look at 1 Corinthians 13:4-7:

> Love is patient, love is kind. It does not envy, it does not boast, it is not proud. It does not dishonor others, it is not self-seeking, it is not easily angered, it keeps no record of wrongs. Love does not delight in evil but rejoices with the truth. It always protects, always trusts, always hopes, always perseveres.

When you read these verses, what do you think some good friendship qualities are? Putting the verse into your own words, take a moment and describe what the Bible says about being a good and loving friend:

_____

_____

_____

_____

_____

Now, think about your own friendships. Do these words describe most of your friends? Do they describe *you* as a friend? God's Word gives us the truth about being a friend and helps us see if we need to be a better friend ourselves or maybe find some kinder friends.

And what about obeying your parents? (Hey, I heard that groan!) Here's what God's Word says about *that*:

> Children, obey your parents in everything, for this pleases the Lord (Colossians 3:20).

When should you obey your parents? _____

_____

And *why* should you obey them? _____

_____

Let's look at just one more example. What about working hard and doing your best? Colossians 3:23-24 says:

> Whatever you do, work at it with all your heart, as working for the Lord, not for human masters, since you know that you will receive an inheritance from the Lord as a reward. It is the Lord Christ you are serving.

Once again, put this verse into your own words and write down what God is telling you about working hard and doing your best:

_____

_____

_____

The Bible gives you very clear truth on what to do, how to do it, and when to do it. It's basically a guidebook to living your life. I'm so thankful God has given us the Bible because without it, I would totally fail life's true or false test!

✳ God's Love and the Truth

Another cool thing about the truth is that not only do you have the Bible helping you know what to do and how to live, but you also have God Himself guiding you every day! He does this when you pray and He listens to and answers your prayers. He also helps you through other people who care about you. God's Word says we need each other:

> Two are better than one, because they have a good return for their labor: If either of them falls down, one can help the other up (Ecclesiastes 4:9-10).

Isn't that great to know? That's why it's so important to have good Christian friends so you can help each other. Maybe you and your BFF are hanging out with another girl who is sometimes mean to other kids. Together, you and your BFF can tell that girl, "Hey, what you said wasn't very nice. We like you, but we don't like spending time with you when you act that way." And then keep showing that girl—and everyone else—kindness so she knows how to be nice to others. It's so much easier with a friend beside you!

God gives us the truth because He loves us so much. He wants our lives to be filled with joy and happiness and all good things. Yep, once again it all comes down to God's love for you and how worth it you are to Him!

You are forever loved by God. Completely loved by God! When you understand this, you can trust Him in a way you never have before. And you can trust that He will give you His truth, which is the *real* truth. God's love completely realized in your heart completely changes your life.

Once you realize how much you're worth to your heavenly Father, you'll stop obsessing over every little mistake you make. You'll stop comparing yourself to your siblings or your friends or other girls. You'll love who you really are. You'll live with a smile on your face and happiness in your heart.

When the great Scottish preacher and author George Mac-Donald—who wrote some really wonderful children's books— was trying to explain God's incredible love to his son, the boy replied that such a thing sounded too good to be true. "Nay, laddie, it's just so good it *must* be true."

I love that image of God's love—*so good it must be true*. His love is truth!

❋ DISCOVER YOUR WORTH ❋

God's gift of love is a total surprise. Better than a huge birthday present you totally weren't expecting but received anyway. Better than a "just because" gift from your friend. Better than the most awesome birthday party treat bag ever. All you need to do is receive it, accept it, thank Him that He thinks you're worth it, and then start blessing others with love and kindness.

God's Word Says You're Worth It

"Then you will know the truth, and the truth will set you free" (John 8:32).

The best thing about truth is the freedom that comes with it. Freedom to live as Jesus wants you to live. Freedom to trust God and not worry about stuff. Freedom to be who you are and do what you love and have fun living your life. Freedom to walk with God!

When You Need to Forgive

*If we confess our sins, he is faithful
and just and will forgive us our sins
and purify us from all unrighteousness.*

1 JOHN 1:9

Amanda folded her arms and glared down at her little brother. "There's no way it was an accident!" she said firmly. "You ruined my new gymnastics bag with those markers, and now I have to go to practice with it looking all nasty."

"I said I was sorry!" Six-year-old Emmett started to cry.

"Amanda and Emmett! What's going on in here?" Their mom stepped into the room. "I can hear you all the way out in the garden."

"Emmett colored all over my new gymnastics bag and it's ruined! He said he was sorry," Amanda said, continuing to glare at her little brother, "but that doesn't really help. The markers won't wash out, and now I have to take it to practice looking like this."

Emmett ran out of the room, sobbing.

"I'm sorry this happened, Amanda, and I think Emmett

truly is sorry too. We'll see what we can do about replacing your gymnastics bag, but right now I'm more worried about you and your brother. Did you tell him you forgave him?"

"No way!" said Amanda. "I'm still too mad at him to forgive him."

"Well, we're going to need to work on that one before we even start talking about a new gymnastics bag. Why don't you come help me in the garden and we can talk a little more."

✾ ✾ ✾

orgiveness. It's hard, even when you know it's the right thing to do. And even if it's something you learned about a long time ago.

When you were little, one of the first things you were probably taught was to say, "I'm sorry." These are two of the best words to know! And there are three other words that are also important to learn: "I forgive you." They go hand in hand with "I'm sorry."

It sounds pretty simple, but forgiveness is a super hard thing! One day when my son Christian was little, he asked me how much was 70 times 7. I replied that it was 490 and asked him why he wanted to know.

"My teacher says that we have to forgive that many times," he answered.

"Yes, that's true, Christian."

"But after 490 times, I don't have to forgive any more, right?"

Okaaay...he made me think there! I explained that we need to forgive others as God forgives us—and that we need forgiveness way, way more than 490 times. That wasn't the answer my son was looking for, though. He told me he was sure he couldn't forgive one of his classmates that many times. I'm not sure what the classmate had done, but obviously Christian was pretty unhappy with him.

I can think of some people in my life like Christian's classmate. Can you? What about those mean girls at school? Or the teacher who yelled at the entire class, even though it was only one kid who was goofing around? Or the bully who always puts people down? These people have hurt us, and we don't like it. We don't really want to see them or talk to them...and we *really* don't want to forgive them!

When I'm feeling like this, I stop and remind myself that I've been forgiven by God way more often than I've had to forgive others. If 490 had been God's max with me, I would have gone beyond that number a long time ago!

❋ How Do You Forgive?

When we don't feel like forgiving, we need to look in the mirror and thank God that we're looking back at a fully forgiven person. God has forgiven you—every time, for everything! So it's our job to go and do likewise. We're supposed to be like Jesus, and that includes forgiving others.

But it's sooooo hard! I can hear you saying. *They don't care that they've hurt me, and anyway, I don't even feel like forgiving them.*

The word *feel* is important here. When we decide to forgive someone, we need to ignore our feelings about them. We can still see all of their faults—and choose to avoid that person if we don't feel safe around them—but we need to forgive by *faith*, not by *feeling*. By faith we say, "I let go of what you did to me. It doesn't matter how I feel. I forgive you just as God forgave me." And then you let it go, like releasing a helium-filled balloon. You watch and watch as the balloon floats away, but eventually it's gone. You aren't holding on to it anymore, and it's no longer a part of your world.

Can you think of anyone you need to forgive? Has someone done something to you—like Amanda's brother did to her—and you haven't been able to forgive them yet? Take a minute to write down what happened here:

_____

_____

_____

_____

_____

You can pray about it right now, and you can keep coming back to this page and praying about it until you're able to forgive. God is patient with you, and sometimes you need to be patient with yourself. You'll get there!

The main reason to forgive others is because God tells us we should. But there's another amazing side to forgiveness. When we let go of our feelings of anger and frustration, we feel better. It hurts to be mad at someone. All those bad feelings take up our energy. They can even cause us to lose sleep and get sick. God made forgiveness a two-way street—forgiveness helps others *and* it helps you!

✿ You've Got This!

I've met so many people who have trouble forgiving. It doesn't matter who hurt them—a friend, a family member, or maybe even someone they don't really know.

What we all need to realize here is that God has totally forgiven us for our sins. God has told us, "It's okay. I forgive you!" And He's done this hundreds and hundreds and hundreds of times—way more than 490!

So you can do it! God did it, and He can show you how. You've got this!

Now, I know how hard it is to forgive someone who has been mean to you. It's hard to forgive someone who makes fun of you. It's hard to forgive someone who talks about you behind your back. I get it! But God's love and grace make it possible for you to forgive.

When you forgive someone who has been making you feel worthless, you take a big step closer to seeing how much worth you have in God's eyes. Forgiveness helps you see yourself more clearly. Forgiveness helps you like yourself more. Forgiveness brings you closer to God.

And God is there to help you every step of the way! First Peter 5:7 says, "Cast all your anxiety on him because he cares for you." God *promises* He cares. God *promises* He will be with you. And He never, ever breaks His promises. I love that—and everything else—about Him.

❊ Time to Forgive!

Okay, you know what forgiveness is. You know you should forgive. You know what happens when you *don't* forgive. So now you've arrived at the moment of forgiveness. But…how?

When you're struggling to forgive someone, try to step outside of your own life and put yourself in the other person's shoes. I've found this to be really helpful when I'm having trouble forgiving someone. Maybe I don't really understand what's going on in that person's life. The mean girl at school may get yelled at all the time at home, so she goes to school and picks on other kids. The boy who's always making fun of the way you do everything may be under a lot of pressure from his parents. The teacher who always seems grumpy may be taking care of her sick father. You just never know.

After you've tried putting yourself in the other person's shoes, it's time to move on to the actual forgiving part. Take a deep breath. Here we go!

First, start off with today. Don't think about what happened yesterday. Don't think about what may happen tomorrow. Stick with right now. And then tell *everything* to God. Don't leave anything out! Nothing is going to be a surprise, after all. He knows exactly what happened, and He's ready to listen to you.

Next, don't focus on blaming the person you're forgiving.

Instead, tell God that you've had trouble forgiving this person and letting go of what happened.

Finally, tell Him, "I'm sorry I haven't forgiven this person until now. Please forgive me for still being upset with them."

You've done it! You've forgiven!

DO I HAVE TO FORGIVE IN PERSON?

Sometimes it's the right thing to forgive someone in person. When someone tells you, "I'm sorry," the best thing to do is to say, "I forgive you." Say it right then and there, even if you don't feel like it. Remember, forgiveness is about *faith*, not *feelings*.

Other times, you can tell the person "I forgive you" even if they didn't tell you they were sorry! This takes a lot of courage, but it's super powerful. It can change their heart as well as your own heart.

And, finally, there are the times when you can tell God you forgive someone and you can forgive them in your heart without ever speaking to them in person. Maybe you don't see the person anymore. Maybe—like in the case of a bully—the safe thing to do is avoid them. Maybe it just never works out to talk face-to-face. You can still forgive them, and God will completely understand.

❋ DISCOVER YOUR WORTH ❋

Maybe you've talked to God over and over about the *things* someone did to hurt you...but have you talked about the *person* to Him? Have you made it all about you, or have you stopped to consider the other person? If you haven't, start praying for that person until you feel your heart changing toward them. Keep praying until you feel like you want good things to happen in their life. And keep praying until you can actually smile when you think of that person. It might sound totally crazy right now, but with God all things are possible. Forgiveness is worth it!

God's Word Says You're Worth It

"Therefore, as God's chosen people, holy and dearly loved, clothe yourselves with compassion, kindness, humility, gentleness and patience. Bear with each other and forgive one another if any of you has a grievance against someone. Forgive as the Lord forgives you" (Colossians 3:12-13).

The Bible tells us how important it is to forgive others. God truly cares that we get along with other people and that we are kind to each other. He knows that we need each other! And that's why forgiveness is so important. We're all worth so much to Him—and we're worth it to each other.

8

God Changes You and Your Life

*If anyone is in Christ, the
new creation has come:
The old has gone, the new is here!*

2 CORINTHIANS 5:17

"Hang on a sec! Let me find a pair of shorts!" Olivia called to her dad as she frantically searched the piles on her floor for her favorite pair of track shorts. Where were those blue ones? Was that them? Nope. That was the sundress she'd worn to church yesterday. What about that? Her swimsuit cover-up. Well, she was finding things—but not what she was looking for.

"Laurel, have you seen my blue track shorts?" Olivia asked her older sister. "I wanted to wear them to the lake, and I have no idea where they are."

Laurel surveyed the mountain of clothing—along with books and games and shoes—on Olivia's floor. "I'm surprised you can find anything in this mess!"

"Hey!" retorted Olivia. "I cleaned up on Saturday. It's just that we've been going so many places, I have to keep changing my clothes. After church we went swimming at the pool. And then we went on that bike ride. And there was the birthday party. Plus, it's been really cold in the mornings. I can't help it!"

"Is that them?" Laurel pointed at a hint of blue hiding in the mess of Olivia's covers.

"Oh, yeah. Thanks, Laurel!" Olivia grabbed her shorts and pulled them on, tossing her pajama pants on the floor. She'd pick them up tonight...or maybe tomorrow morning. Right now she needed to finish changing for the lake trip.

❋ ❋ ❋

Have you ever had those days when you change your clothes a lot? Maybe the outfit you laid out the night before didn't quite work for today's weather, so you had to change it. Then you wanted to put on shorts and a T-shirt right after school, so you changed again. And you forgot that your family was going out to a nice dinner for your brother's birthday, which means—you got it!—more changing. At the end of the day, all that changing adds up...to a giant mess on your floor!

And you'll eventually need to deal with all those changes. You'll need to sort things out, put things away, and tidy things up—or else you'll never be able to find anything ever again.

Did you know other types of changes are happening in your life? As you're learning more about God and growing in Him, your life and your heart are changing. But not totally all at once. When God changes your life, your old thoughts and habits don't magically disappear. They don't hop in the washing machine all by themselves or fold themselves up and jump back into your drawers. (You probably wouldn't want them back, anyway!) You might think that they're gone for good, but you can find an old thought hanging around in your mind just like you find a smelly sock hiding at the bottom of your back-pack. You thought you'd gotten rid of it, and finding it is no fun—it stinks. Literally!

CHANGING TIME!

Just for fun, take a look at how many times you changed your clothes this past week. Write down the activities you had every day ("school," "volleyball," or even "sleep") and see how that laundry all adds up. (You can show this to your mom when she complains about all that laundry!)

SUNDAY: _____

MONDAY: _____

TUESDAY: _____

WEDNESDAY: _____

THURSDAY: _____

FRIDAY: _____

SATURDAY: _____

Sometimes it's really hard to change your old thoughts and habits. Even though God is helping you, other things in your life can make that change hard. Sometimes there's a lot of pressure to be like other kids and do what they're doing, even if you know those things are wrong. It can be super hard not to go back to your old thoughts and habits and actions when the people around you aren't living for Jesus. But keep at it! God will help you make changes that last because He knows you can do it!

✻ Not Feeling Worth It

Have you ever had something embarrassing happen to you that was basically impossible to forget about? Even when things happen that aren't our fault, it's hard to push those moments out of our memory. Or maybe you did something wrong and you *did* realize it—like hanging out with a group of friends who make comments and jokes that hurt other kids' feelings. Since then, you've gotten to know Jesus and realized He doesn't want you acting that way. So you've prayed about it and made some changes. You've started hanging out with a nicer group of friends—and maybe you've even apologized to the kids you were mean to. But you still feel bad about what happened. And you wonder if other people realize you're not the same person you used to be. You wonder if you're really worth it.

Don't spend too much time thinking about this. Yes, it's important to ask for forgiveness. Yes, it's important to understand that God wants you to show love and kindness to others and to do the right thing. But you also need to just move on. God has great stuff in store for you, and He wants you to focus on your awesome future!

✳ People Pleaser

Have you ever heard of a "people pleaser"? It's someone who is so focused on making other people happy that they kind of forget about themselves. Not that it's a bad thing to make others happy, but sometimes you can worry way too much about what other people think—so much that you lose track of what *really* matters.

Did you know you can try too hard to please God as well? I know this may sound kind of crazy, but it's true!

When I was younger, I was super concerned about pleasing God. Obsessed with it, actually. I was determined to become the perfect Christian girl. I thought if I did everything perfectly, God would continue to love me. And I also thought if I did something wrong, God would be mad at me. I couldn't stand to have anyone angry with me, so I tried very hard to please God in every way I could think of. And I didn't just try to please God. I tried to please people too. If other people were happy with me, I could be happy with myself. If other people were disappointed in me, I was disappointed in myself. And I believed (even though it wasn't true) that God was also disappointed in me.

Let me tell you, this is *not* a good way to live! It's not going to make you feel good about yourself. It's not going to make you feel good about others. And it's not going to help you grow in your relationship with God.

WHO ARE YOU TRYING TO PLEASE?

Who in your life are you trying to please? Who do you worry about making happy? Circle all the people who apply:

parents	friends	teachers	coaches
grandparents	cousins	Sunday school teacher	
youth leader	God	yourself	

No matter how perfect you are, you're never going to be able to please everyone. While you should show love and kindness to everyone in your life, you shouldn't spend all your time worrying about making everyone happy. God loves you and accepts you, and He will always show you the right thing to do when you choose to follow Him.

✳ Real Change

When was Olivia ready to go to the lake? Was it when her sister Laurel found her blue track shorts? Not quite! Olivia first had to take off her pajama pants and then put on her shorts before she was ready. She had to *change*.

But knowing when your heart is changed isn't always quite

as easy as changing your clothes. You can't look in the mirror and see your heart! God sees your heart, though, and He promises that if you follow Him, your heart will be changed. The Bible says, "I will give them a heart to know me, that I am the LORD. They will be my people, and I will be their God, for they will return to me with all their heart" (Jeremiah 24:7).

If you stick with God—if you read your Bible and pray and follow Him—He promises to change your heart and your life. This change will be amazing and real—and it will last forever!

❉ DISCOVER YOUR WORTH ❉

Sometimes things that happened to you in the past still affect your today and tomorrow. Maybe you broke your arm when you were little, and it never quite healed right. Or you were really mean to your former best friend, and she still won't speak to you even though you've said you're sorry. Or you tried to paint a mural on your bedroom wall and messed up, and your parents haven't gotten around to repainting your room. You can give what happened to God, but it still made a mark on who you are (or on where you live, as in the case of your room). And that's okay. That's part of changing and growing and becoming more like Jesus.

God's Word Says You're Worth It

"Brothers and sisters, I do not consider myself yet to have taken hold of it. But one thing I do: Forgetting what is behind and straining toward what is ahead, I press on toward the goal to win the prize for which God has called me heavenward in Christ Jesus" (Philippians 3:13-14).

When you change your clothes, you're looking ahead to your next activity—school or playing outside or going to church or whatever you're doing next. In the Bible, God encourages us to look ahead and keep our eyes focused on the big "what's next"—that amazing place called heaven!

9

God Sees Your Heart

*Above all else, guard your heart,
for everything you do flows from it.*
PROVERBS 4:23

"I call the top bunk!" Kendra tossed her sleeping bag and pillow onto the rickety camp bunk bed as her best friend, Amelia, laughed and set her things on the lower bunk.

"You're probably going to fall off your bed when you're asleep," Amelia said.

"Yeah, probably!" Kendra giggled. "Hey, are those our counselors out there? I don't recognize any of them from last year."

"Me either," said Amelia, peering through the window. "I bet that blond girl with the ponytail is a soccer player. She's wearing soccer shorts."

"And that short girl has to be a cheerleader or a gymnast," guessed Kendra.

"And the tall one with the glasses is probably really smart and doesn't play sports," added Amelia.

Later on, at campfire, the college-age counselors introduced themselves.

"I'm Megan," said the blond girl. "I'm in the gospel choir at my college."

"Hey, everyone!" said the short girl. "My name is Nicole, and I play basketball."

The tall girl with glasses stood up. "Hi, campers! I'm Carmen, and I'm on the lacrosse team at my school."

"We were totally wrong!" whispered Kendra.

"I know!" said Amelia. "I guess you can't tell who someone is just by what they look like or what they're wearing."

✿ ✿ ✿

It's totally natural to look at a person and try to figure out what they're like based on how they look and what they're wearing. Kendra and Amelia were excited to meet their new camp counselors, and they guessed some things about them—but they were totally wrong! When we're trying to figure out other people based on just a few observations, sometimes we may be right, but more often we're wrong. And that's okay. What we look like on the outside shouldn't really be that important. After all, it's not that important to God.

The Bible talks about this a lot. When Samuel the prophet was looking at a group of brothers to decide who would be the future king of Israel, he thought it was Eliab that God had chosen, but instead God told him, "Do not consider his appearance or his height, for I have rejected him. The LORD does not look at the things people look at. People look at the outward appearance, but the LORD looks at the heart" (1 Samuel 16:7).

INSIDE OR OUTSIDE?

When you're looking for a good friend, you might have a list of qualities that are important to you. Which of these things do you look for in a friend? Check the ones that apply.

_____ She is kind to people.

_____ She wears cool clothes.

_____ She lives in a big house.

_____ She likes to do the same things I do.

_____ She loves Jesus.

_____ She is popular at school.

_____ She makes me laugh.

_____ She does nice things for others.

_____ She is smart.

_____ She tries to do the right thing.

Do you think that the things you marked are the same ones God would mark? When you're making friends, it's important that you "click" and get along with them, but what they're like on the inside is what's most important.

In the New Testament, the apostle Peter reminds women, "Your beauty should not come from outward adornment, such as elaborate hairstyles and the wearing of gold jewelry or fine clothes. Rather, it should be that of your inner self, the unfading beauty of a gentle and quiet spirit, which is of great worth in God's sight (1 Peter 3:3-4).

God doesn't care if you're tall or short. He doesn't care if you have straight hair or curly hair. He doesn't care if you have brand-name jeans or no-name hand-me-downs. He doesn't care if you have braces or glasses. Those things don't really matter to Him. What's important to God is who you are on the inside and what your heart looks like.

God cares that you are truthful. He cares that you are kind. He cares that you are giving. He cares that you are humble. He cares that you are thoughtful. When God looks at you, those are the things He sees first.

✿ Just the Way You Are

Throughout this book, we've been talking about being worth it. It's important to know that your worth—your real, true value—is from God and God alone. That's hard to understand when we live in a world that puts so much focus on what we look like and what we accomplish. But God doesn't care if the world says you're pretty. God doesn't care if the world says you're smart. God doesn't care if the world says you're popular. God doesn't care if the world says you're perfect because guess what? There's no such thing as perfect!

The truth is that perfection is a myth, pure and simple. It

doesn't exist in this world. Godly beauty, though, is a truth that never fades. When I read that beauty that comes from within is precious to God, I want that. Don't you? I want to live a life that brings God honor and pleasure. When God looks at me—at the *entire* me, which includes what's inside—I want Him to be happy with what He sees. I want Him to realize who I am and say, "You're perfect just the way you are." And He does!

But it's soooo hard not to fall into the trap of our worth being based on things that don't really matter. Like what kind of grades we get. Or what brand of jeans we wear. Or how good of an artist we are. Or how many friends we have. Or how talented we are at sports or music.

None of these things matter to God.

Once you start looking at yourself as God sees you, you'll realize that too. And that makes life so much better! You stop worrying about yourself and your own stuff and start focusing on other people. Let me tell you something. Forgetting about yourself is one of the best ways to become beautiful in the true sense of the word.

Think about it this way. If you obsess about your braces or your glasses or the zits you may be starting to get and constantly complain about those things, what do you think others will see when they look at you? Yep, that's right—braces and glasses and zits! But if you stop feeling sorry for yourself and start focusing on being a good friend or doing nice things for others, what do you think people will see? They'll see a girl with a good heart—someone positive and kind and caring who would be an awesome friend to have!

God wants you to be content with yourself just the way you

are. Sure, you can be happy when your braces are removed. Or when you get a new pair of designer jeans for Christmas. Or when you get first place in the art competition. But you should be happiest when you know you're changing on the inside and becoming more like Jesus.

❉ No Secrets

Some secrets are good—like the room redo your parents did while you were at summer camp or the surprise party you're planning for your sister's birthday. But a lot of the time, secrets aren't good. Like when you see two girls whispering together and looking at you. When you ask them what they're talking about and they say, "Oh, it's a secret," how does that make you feel? Probably a little scared that they were talking about *you*, right?

The nice thing about God seeing your heart is that He knows exactly who you are and what you've done. You don't have to keep any secrets from Him. When you ask Him to help you change, you don't have to explain to Him what you want to change. He already knows!

Maybe you've been talking badly about others behind their back. Maybe you're starting to care too much about what you look like. Maybe you've gotten into the bad habit of arguing with your parents—about everything, even things that don't really matter. Now is the time to tell God, "You know who I've been and how I've been acting. I don't want to be like that anymore. Please help me to become a better person and to become more like You. You tell me I'm worth it, so I believe You will help me!"

GOOD SECRETS AND BAD SECRETS

Sometimes it can be hard to know if a secret is good or bad. Let's look at a few examples:

A. Your friend Grace tells you that your friend Erica's parents are getting divorced, and that's why Erica has been so sad lately. She says she knows it's okay to share it with you because you're good at keeping secrets.

Good or bad? _____

B. Your mom is having trouble figuring out what to get your brother for his birthday, and she knows you may have some good ideas. She has you write down the ideas and tells you to please keep it secret from your brother.

Good or bad? _____

C. Your friend Ella tells you she knows the answers to tomorrow's math test because her older sister took the exact same test last year and still has the paper. Ella says, "You can look at the answers if you want to, but don't tell the teacher I have them. You have to keep it a secret if you want to be my friend!"

Good or bad? _____

Did you choose? Okay, now let's go through the answers:

A. This one's a little tricky. Even though both you and Grace care about Erica and have been worried about her, this secret is still bad. You don't know for certain that Erica's parents are getting a divorce because you haven't heard anything from Erica herself. You should tell Grace, "Erica hasn't told me anything, so I don't know if this is true or not. Please tell her she can talk to me, but unless she tells me something, I'm going to pretend I didn't hear this."

B. This is a good secret! The end result is going to be a happy brother with terrific birthday presents (because you're great at figuring out what to get him). If you tell your brother what you're getting him, you'll disappoint your mom and it will be a letdown for your brother when he opens his gifts. Keep this secret!

C. This is definitely a bad secret! Ella is planning to cheat, which means she won't learn the math and may ruin her relationship with her teacher and get Ella in trouble—and you don't want to be any part of it. This is when you need to stand up for yourself and say, "Ella, I'm not going to cheat. If you want to cheat, you can, but you know you shouldn't. And if you do, I'm going to have to tell the teacher because it's not fair to the rest of us."

How we acted and what we did in the past—whether good or bad—is just a road behind us that has led us to today. All of our roads probably look different, but they're all designed to turn our hearts toward Jesus. No, God doesn't want bad things to happen to us. No, He doesn't want us to do bad things. But He does want everything that happens to lead us to Him because it's there—and *only* there—that we find our true worth.

Of course, it would be nice to learn that we're worth it without having to go through tough stuff! It would be nice to have avoided that mean girl and still learned what makes a true friend. It would be nice to have avoided that broken leg and still learned how to be patient when you can't play the sport you love. It would be nice to have avoided that bad grade and still learned that a perfect report card doesn't make you a perfect person. But sometimes we need to learn these lessons the hard way!

God cares deeply about you. And He knows what it's going to take for you to learn and grow and become more like Him. He sees exactly who you are, and He knows that someday you'll look back at your life and say, "Wow! God really *was* with me the whole time. He knew exactly what I needed all along. I must definitely be worth it to Him!"

❋ DISCOVER YOUR WORTH ❋

When you're talking to God about changing your heart and making you more like Him, you can say:

Dear Lord, I take everything to You. I hand every experience over to You. It's not in my life anymore. It's not important. It doesn't have any effect on who I am now and who I will be in the future. Thank You for loving me and forgiving me and turning all things into something good. In Jesus' name. Amen.

God's Word Says You're Worth It

"Nothing in all creation is hidden from God's sight. Everything is uncovered and laid bare before the eyes of him to whom we must give account" (Hebrews 4:13).

God sees everything! This might seem scary when we think of the times we've messed up or done something wrong, but it's actually a very good thing. He knows us so well. And He loves us and is always there to help us learn and grow and become more like Him.

10

When Things Don't Go Your Way

"I know the plans I have for you," declares the LORD, "plans to prosper you and not to harm you, plans to give you a hope and a future."

JEREMIAH 29:11

"Are you sure we're going the right way?" Sarah asked from the backseat. "I don't remember this road."

"Well, that's the way the GPS is telling me to go," said her mom.

"Wait a sec," said her brother, Justin, who was navigating from the front passenger seat. "It says it's recalculating."

"Again?" replied their mom. "I don't know if we're ever going to find the lake!"

Sarah, her mom, and her brother had all decided to drop everything and head for the lake on one of the final days of summer vacation. Their paddleboard was strapped on top of the car and their inflatable kayaks and paddles were stuffed in the back. Her mom hadn't bothered looking up directions to the lake because...well, that's what the GPS was for!

Unless the GPS had no clue which way to go—like right now.

"Um, I think we turn on this road." Sarah's mom bit her lip and flipped on the car's left turn signal. As soon as she turned, they heard the familiar voice coming from the phone: "Recalculating."

Sarah sighed and slumped down in her seat. It was getting hot out, and she was ready to jump in the water. Were they ever going to find the lake?

✳ ✳ ✳

Have you ever taken a look at where you're headed and asked yourself, *Am I going the right way? Is this where I want to be right now? Am I doing what I think I should be doing?*

These may sound like some pretty grown-up questions—like you may need to be old enough to drive a car in order to answer them—but they're actually really important things to ask yourself now. Maybe you thought you'd have another best friend after your last one moved away. Maybe you thought you'd be able to play that hard song on your violin or have mastered that back handspring in gymnastics—and you still can't do it. Maybe you thought you'd know God a little better. And maybe you're a little bit disappointed where you are in your life right now.

Are you where you thought you'd be—and where you'd hoped to be—at this point in your life?

If not, take a lesson from the GPS voice Sarah heard when she and her mom and brother were trying to find the lake. Remember what it was saying? "Recalculating!"

Now, why was the voice on the GPS saying that? It's because the driver—Sarah's mom—had taken a wrong turn. And to get back where she needed to go, the GPS had to redirect her back onto the right path.

Just as Sarah knew their final destination was the lake, God knows our final destination. And no matter how many "wrong turns" we make, God can "recalculate" our journey so that we're soon right back where we're supposed to be. What's so great about this is that when you accept God's destination and get on His path, you're no longer disappointed about where you are in life. Things that you thought mattered a lot don't really matter anymore. When you have faith that God is your GPS, you follow His directions and get excited about your destination!

God will always, always work out the details of your life so that you get where you're supposed to go. Now, this may not be where you think you *should* go or where you think you want to go, but it's the place God has chosen for you to go. And it's always even better than your original plan!

❀ A Better Plan

Sometimes we're scared to go where God is leading us. It's only natural to be afraid of change. It's normal to be freaked out about doing something different. You may be happy in private school, but your family can't afford to pay for it anymore, and now you're totally terrified about going to public school. Or your best friend moved away, and you're scared that if you make a new best friend, she'll move away too.

Life doesn't always go the way we'd planned. So many things can pop into your path and change your course. But one important part of growing up and getting closer to God is dealing with the fact that our Plan A might not even be God's Plan Z. It can be super hard to accept the unexpected twists and turns on the road of life.

While it's great to have hopes and dreams and plans and expectations, don't be too disappointed if those things don't happen. It doesn't mean you did something wrong. It just means that God wants to take you somewhere else.

So try to be thankful that your expectations were unmet. If you stayed in private school, maybe you wouldn't figure out that you really loved science and might want to become a doctor someday. If you spent too much time being sad about your best friend moving away, you may have missed out on some great friendships. You just never know!

THE FUTURE ME!

Just for fun, write down where you see yourself in the future. Where are you living? What are you doing? What do you think you'll be like?

In one year, I'll be _____ years old and I see myself...

_____

_____

In five years, I'll be _____ years old and I see myself...

_____

_____

In ten years, I'll be _____ years old and I see myself...

_____

_____

Someday it will be fun to look back at your answers and see if you guessed right!

❋ If Only…

Dreams that don't come true and plans that don't work out can make us feel really sad. You can look back at a diary or a journal or pictures and think about what might have been, something I call the *if only* syndrome…

If only I hadn't had that teacher.
If only I had made different friends.
If only my family hadn't moved to another state.
If only I had worked harder in that class.
If only I hadn't wasted so much of my summer being lazy.

But don't look back! It doesn't matter what already happened. It *does* matter what is going to happen. The Bible is filled with stories of men and women with dreams that didn't come true and plans that never worked out. Life didn't go like they'd planned for it to go, but it *did* go the way God wanted it to go. And that's what matters!

❋ Saying Yes

If you're feeling disappointed a lot of the time, ask yourself how much you're listening to God and how much you're saying yes to the things He's asking you to do. I've learned that happiness and satisfaction come from saying yes to God. And saying yes to God sometimes means saying yes to some things we'd rather say no to. Like saying yes to the friend group you have, not the friend group you think you want to have. Saying yes to playing with your baby sister while your mom cooks dinner.

THAT'S NOT FAIR!

You're going to have times in your life when things seem totally unfair.

- The mean girl who talks about everyone behind their back and loves to leave people out gets voted classroom president. You were totally nice to everyone—and you lost the election to that girl.

- The kid who cheats on every test and copies other students' homework gets all A's. You studied super hard for the tests and did all the homework on your own—and you got a B in the class.

- The teammate who skips practice and doesn't try very hard gets first place all-around at your gymnastics meet. You went to every gymnastics practice and worked your tail off—and you fell on the balance beam and didn't win.

These things seem totally unfair, huh? But trust God that these things happened for a reason and that He knows what He's doing—because He does! Your part is to give Him your heart, your faith, and your life. Say yes to His plan for you. Don't worry about fairness or keeping score or any of that. Instead, live your life the way God wants you to. It's so much better that way!

Saying yes to practicing the piano before going outside to play with your friends.

When you're first learning how to do this, it may feel a little bit like life isn't fair. Like it's not fair you have to practice piano when your friends can start playing right away. But what we think of as fairness and what God sees as fairness don't always look the same. This can be hard to understand, but it's true. When things don't seem fair, we need to remember that God is good and that He never makes mistakes. Remember, you can always trust God to be there for you when you say yes to Him!

I love what Psalm 62:5 tells me: "Yes, my soul, find rest in God; my hope comes from him." The main thing in life you need to do is listen to God and do what He asks. He'll take care of the rest!

❋ DISCOVER YOUR WORTH ❋

When things you thought or hoped would happen in your life either didn't happen the way you wanted them to or didn't happen at all, it's time to pray about it. Ask God to help you know what to do when life isn't going the way you wanted it to. He will help you see what His expectations and plans are for your life, and you'll be excited to see all the amazing things He has in store for you!

God's Word Says You're Worth It

"We know that in all things God works for the good of those who love him, who have been called according to his purpose" (Romans 8:28).

It's never too early to learn that God is going to make everything work out okay in the end. No matter what's worrying you or scaring you or frustrating you right now, as long as you love God, He's got this! Nothing is too big for Him. Nothing is too hard for Him. Your future is in His capable hands. How wonderful is that?

Jesus Has a Plan for Your Future

Do not let not your hearts be troubled.
You believe in God; believe also in me.
My Father's house has many rooms; if it
were not so, would I have told you that I
am going there to prepare a place for you?
And if I go and prepare a place for you,
I will come back and take you to be with
me that you also may be where I am.

JOHN 14:1-3

"Okay, you can open your eyes now!" Taylor's mom said.

Taylor blinked. Wow! Was this really her room? While she'd been away at her grandparents' house over spring break, her parents had redone her room. And just look at it now!

The walls were painted a restful mint green. Gone was the bright yellow color along with the Winnie the Pooh stickers she'd plastered all over the walls when she was little. The stained carpet had been pulled up to reveal hardwood floors, cozied up by several fluffy white rugs. Her bed, dresser, and bookcase had been painted a glossy white. The special pink-and-mint green quilt Taylor's great-grandmother had made and her favorite stuffed animals made the bed look so welcoming.

Most of the stuff in her room was the same, but just a few changes made such a difference. And her parents had worked so hard!

"Thanks, Mom and Dad!" Taylor said, hugging them both. "I can't believe this is really my room!"

* * *

Taylor was pretty excited about her room redo. It *would* be fun to walk into a space prepared just for you, wouldn't it?

Did you know that Jesus has an awesome place prepared just for you? He does—it's called heaven! He's spared no expense, He's made it perfect just for you, and He's so excited for you to see it someday. You're so worth it! He wouldn't do such a thing for someone who has no worth.

We tend to forget about the future as we concentrate on what's happening right now in our daily lives. And that makes sense. When you're dealing with homework and fights between friends and after-school activities, it can be hard to think about tomorrow or next week or next month...let alone *eternity*! And eternity—you know, the *forever* that will happen someday—is a pretty hard thing to grasp. But you need to start telling yourself that you're living this right-now life in preparation for eternity.

Remember, your true identity is God's beloved child. The best way to understand this is to believe that God's love for you will never change even if things change in your life. And things *will* change. Your friendships will change. Your teachers will change. Your interests will change. Your body will change. Your emotions will change. Change isn't necessarily a bad thing—it's just different. And different can be scary, even if the change is good.

✻ Your Eternal Future

When you're dealing with change, it's nice to know that God's love for you will never, ever change. I try to remember this as I keep my focus on God and my future—my *eternal* future. When you keep your eyes focused on eternity, the way you live your life will change. Things like popularity or grades or trophies or possessions won't matter as much. This doesn't mean you should stop trying to be kind to everyone. Or that you shouldn't study or practice hard. It just means you don't need to worry about these things so much.

It takes time to learn to focus on eternity, and God is always patient while we're learning. If your family has a garden, you know what happens when you plant a seed—or, rather, what *doesn't* happen right away. When you plant zucchini seeds in your garden, do you expect to wake up the next morning and find plump, full-grown squashes ready for the picking? Of course not! We all know that growing veggies takes time. So does growth in our spiritual life. And so does developing an understanding of how worth it we are to God.

As you learn and grow and mature in your faith, you're

going to realize more and more how worth it you are to God. And that's just the beginning! Like a plant that's been given plenty of sunlight and water to grow, you'll continue to grow in God's love. As you accept the water of His Word and grow stronger in the sunlight of the Holy Spirit, you'll become changed for the better by God's presence in you. And you'll understand that while the people and places and circumstances in your life will change, God will never change. That's so reassuring to know!

❁ You're God's Masterpiece!

Do you remember how you drew pictures when you were really little? It probably took you about five seconds to create a simple stick figure—and maybe you forgot to add the eyes or hands or feet.

You can think of yourself as a work of art that God is creating—and it's not a simple stick figure, so He can't just scribble it down quickly. God is careful and patient with His creation, just as an artist is careful and patient with the future masterpiece on his easel. And though God may seem slow in His work, He is always present as He works. We are never left alone as His talented hand paints carefully over the canvas of our lives.

When I understood that God was taking His time with me, it changed my life. For so many years I had been doing things for God and failing big time. But when I realized that I actually can't do anything *for* God—and that I can only do things *in* Him—I felt so much better. And I got to know Him better!

God sometimes uses our struggles and our hard times and our bad days to help us get to know Him better. Think about it this way. If you were totally self-confident and thought of yourself as perfect and everything always went your way, would you ever believe that you needed God in your life? Probably not!

IN GOD'S CLASSROOM

I love God, and I love what I'm learning about Him! I may not be in school anymore, but I'm still learning so many things:

- I'm learning to find my worth in God's amazing love for me.
- I'm learning to talk to God about things before I take it out on someone else.
- I'm learning to trust God in all situations, no matter what's happening in my life.
- I'm learning that God is always with me—on the good days and the bad days.
- I'm learning that I matter—that I'm worth it to God!

It's when we go through tough stuff with other people—like a really challenging class with a difficult teacher or a crazy-hard track practice or a canoe trip in a storm during a camping trip—that we really bond with others. Going through tough stuff helps you bond with God.

❋ It All Works Out

Everything happens for a reason. God makes sure of that! He wastes nothing. All that happens in our lives can be redeemed—or made to work out for good. When you read the Bible, you can see that God loves nothing better than to bring good out of really bad situations. When we read the book of Job, we suffer along with him. Pretty much every terrible thing you could ever imagine happens to poor Job.

But then take a look at how the book ends: "The LORD blessed the latter parts of Job's life more than the former part" (Job 42:12). It all turned out okay!

Whatever you've been going through—a tough time at school, family problems, friend drama—please join me in learning a lesson from Job. Our "latter" days—the days from here on out—will be better than yesterday or today. Our best years are coming! We will know our worth as daughters of God, and we will rejoice in it. We will take joy in knowing we were created to love God and give Him pleasure. God wants every one of us to be included in His family.

If you had asked me a while ago what I wanted most, I would have said I wanted to have a heart on fire for God. I didn't want to just gain knowledge about God. I wanted to truly know Him and trust Him with everything. I didn't want to just talk about the love of God. I wanted my life and my heart to be consumed by His love!

That was totally true for me then, and it's totally true for me now.

As we come to the end of this book, here's what I want you to remember: God completely loves and accepts you for who you are. You don't have to act fake or worry about what He thinks or be afraid to be anything but yourself. He sees the real you, and with Him you can be the real you. That's because you're so worth it to Him!

❋ DISCOVER YOUR WORTH ❋

We've had quite a journey together! Right now would be a great time to pray and thank God for taking every situation in your life and using it for good. Ask Him for His help, and then enjoy His peace as you wait for His faithful leading. He holds your future in His hands, and it's exciting for me to think of what He has in store for you. It's all good!

God's Word Says You're Worth It

"Those who hope in the LORD will renew their strength. They will soar on wings like eagles; they will run and not grow weary, they will walk and not be faint"
(Isaiah 40:31).

As you journey through life, remember to keep your focus on the future—it's in God's hands! He has a plan for your life, and He promises to be with you every step of the way. You'll never get tired if you rely on His strength and His power. He promises this!

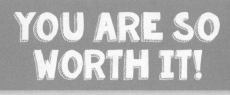

YOU ARE SO WORTH IT!

Glue a picture of yourself here
(or draw one if you like).

Each time you see it, let it remind you
of everything you read in this book
and that you are *so special*—so worth it—to God!